MIND MATTERS

MIND MATTERS

HARPER NORTHWOOD

CONTENTS

1 Introduction   1

2 Understanding the Power of Thoughts   3

3 The Impact of Thoughts on Your Life   5

4 Recognizing Limiting Beliefs   9

5 Overcoming Negative Thought Patterns   11

6 Cultivating Positive Thinking   15

7 Harnessing the Power of Affirmations   19

8 Visualizing Your Desired Future   23

9 The Role of Mindfulness in Transforming Thoughts   27

10 Practicing Gratitude for a Positive Mindset   31

11 Embracing Self-Compassion and Self-Love   33

12 Building Resilience in the Face of Challenges   35

13 Nurturing Healthy Relationships   39

14 Creating a Supportive Environment   43

15 Maintaining Consistency in Thought Transformation   47

16 Taking Action: Applying Mind Transformation Techni
51

CHAPTER 1

Introduction

Welcome to *Mind Matters: Transforming Your Thoughts, Transforming Your Life*, a companion workbook meticulously designed to guide you through a journey of self-discovery and mental transformation. Building upon the principles outlined in the main text *Mind Matters: Overcoming Adversity and Awakening the Self*, this workbook serves as your personal tool for understanding and improving the quality of your thoughts, thereby enhancing your life experiences.

Whether you are seeking personal growth, aiming to help others, or facilitating group or individual coaching sessions, this workbook is an invaluable resource. It provides a systematic approach to comprehending how thoughts shape our realities and offers practical strategies to harness this understanding for a more fulfilling life.

What to Expect

Each chapter in this workbook is crafted to offer:

1. **Concrete Exercises**: Engaging activities to help you become aware of and alter thought patterns.
2. **Practical Applications**: Real-world scenarios and applications to solidify your understanding.

3. **Reflective Questions**: Thought-provoking questions to deepen your self-awareness.
4. **Group Activities**: Exercises designed to facilitate group discussions and collective growth.

Using This Workbook

This workbook is versatile and can be used in conjunction with the main text or as a standalone guide. It is designed to be flexible to fit your personal or group development needs.

The Importance of Thought

At the core of *Mind Matters* is the belief that our individual and collective thinking shapes our world. Negative thoughts, fears, and hatred hinder our ability to create a peaceful and fulfilling life. By transforming our thinking patterns, we can transform our lives and contribute positively to the world around us.

The Journey Ahead

This workbook will equip you with tools to:

- Recognize and understand your thought patterns.
- Implement strategies to direct your thoughts towards positive outcomes.
- Foster a mindset that supports personal and collective growth.

Embark on this journey with an open mind and a willingness to explore the depths of your thoughts. Let this workbook be your guide to a transformed and enriched life.

CHAPTER 2

Understanding the Power of Thoughts

The Effect on Emotions

The link between thought and emotion is a profoundly powerful one. Our thoughts directly influence how we feel. Just imagining a negative event can elicit feelings of anxiety, sadness, anger, or any other emotion associated with that event. The body often cannot distinguish between an imagined scenario and a real one, so repeatedly thinking about a negative experience can make us relive those emotions over and over. This creates a cycle that can be challenging to break. For instance, imagine the impact on your mood if you spend an entire day fixated on failures and disappointments.

On the flip side, positive thinking has the power to elevate our mood. If you're feeling down, acting as if you're happy—by engaging in activities you enjoy and focusing on positive thoughts—can actually make you feel happier. This exercise illustrates the significant power that thoughts have over our emotions.

The Trap of Negative Beliefs

Our thought patterns, when ingrained, can become like tracks that are difficult to deviate from. Innocent-sounding thoughts like "I'm not good enough," "I'm afraid I'll fail," "They won't like me," and "I'm so stupid" can become automatic and go unnoticed. These thoughts, however, shape our perception of the world and can negatively influence how we interpret situations.

For example, if you see life through the lens of "I'm so stupid," even a minor mistake can make you feel like a complete failure. If you believe that you are unlovable or inferior to others, this belief will affect your relationships and prevent others from seeing your best qualities. These negative beliefs can form a self-fulfilling prophecy, where our thoughts create the reality we fear most.

Breaking the Cycle

To transform our lives, it's crucial to become aware of these negative thought patterns and actively work to change them. Here are a few exercises to help:

1. **Awareness Exercise**: Spend a day monitoring your thoughts. Note each negative thought and counter it with a positive one.
2. **Positive Affirmations**: Create a list of positive affirmations and repeat them daily to reinforce a positive mindset.
3. **Mindfulness Practice**: Engage in mindfulness or meditation to help you become aware of your thoughts without judgment.
4. **Journaling**: Write down your thoughts and emotions. This can help you identify patterns and develop strategies to change them.

By consistently practicing these exercises, you can begin to shift your thought patterns towards a more positive and empowering outlook.

CHAPTER 3

The Impact of Thoughts on Your Life

Understanding Thought Patterns

When you enter details in the Thought Catcher, start by focusing on what actually happened, rather than on what you imagined might have happened. This practice encourages realism and helps you spot unreasonable or "time-tangled" thoughts. By comparing these thoughts against the Unhelpful Thinking List, you can develop the skill of identifying and challenging unhelpful thinking styles.

Considering Outcomes

It can be helpful to consider the spectrum of possible outcomes—from the worst to the best and everything in between. Writing in a balanced way can pave the path for new ways of thinking. This exercise encourages you to look at situations from different angles and helps you realize that extreme outcomes are often unlikely.

Identifying Thinking Errors

Reflect on any thinking errors that led to the conclusions recorded in the Thought Catcher. Use the Positive Thoughts Record to weigh the pros and cons of adopting a more balanced perspective. Finish by writing out the balanced thought and contemplating its potential impact on your mood and life over the next week. This practice can help you transition from negative to more constructive thinking patterns.

Impact of Stressful Situations

Problems in life and mood arise not only from stressful situations but also from the thoughts triggered by these events—whether they pertain to the past, present, or future. The Impact of Events Questionnaire (IEQ) will help you pinpoint any upsetting thoughts linked to recent problems. By identifying these thoughts, you can use the Thought Monitoring Record to realistically assess and refine your thought processes, leading to less distressing outcomes.

Evaluating Thought Control

Understanding the effect of unpleasant thoughts and imaginings on your mood can motivate you to take control. The Thought Control Questionnaire is a tool to rate how much you believe in the possibility and worthiness of controlling these thoughts. It can help boost your motivation to learn and apply skills from the Thought Challenging and Behavioral Experiments sections of the workbook.

The Role of Imagery

Unpleasant thoughts often manifest as images in our minds, impacting how we feel. Using the Image Analysis Record, you can learn to identify and alter distressing or unhelpful images to lessen their impact on your mood. This process is akin to the other thought records but focuses on visual elements of thought.

Practical Exercises

Here are some exercises to help you put these principles into practice:

1. **Thought Catcher Exercise**: Note down real events and your thoughts about them. Identify any unhelpful thinking styles.

2. **Positive Thoughts Record**: Counter negative thoughts with positive ones and assess their impact on your mood.
3. **Impact of Events Questionnaire (IEQ)**: Identify and assess the impact of recent problems and your thoughts about them.
4. **Thought Control Questionnaire**: Evaluate your belief in the ability to control thoughts and work towards improving this skill.
5. **Image Analysis Record**: Identify and change distressing images in your mind.

By consistently applying these exercises, you can develop healthier thought patterns and improve your overall mood and life satisfaction.

Recognizing Limiting Beliefs

Identifying Intense Emotional Reactions

Limiting beliefs can often be identified through intense emotional reactions to events. When an event causes strong feelings of anger, frustration, sadness, depression, or anxiety, it is likely connected to a limiting belief. Recognizing these reactions is the first step in uncovering the underlying beliefs that trigger them.

Patterns of Self-Defeating Behaviors

Noticing patterns of self-defeating behaviors is crucial in discovering limiting beliefs. This task can be challenging as many individuals are so accustomed to certain behaviors that they don't recognize them as self-defeating. In such cases, it can be helpful to ask a trusted family member or friend to point out these behaviors.

For instance, someone might frequently search for reasons to be angry because rage has become a comfort zone, stemming from a belief that they must always be tough and never show weakness.

Real-Life Examples

Consider a man who was ridiculed by his father for being too sensitive. As an adult, he struggles to show emotion and affection with his wife and children because he views sensitivity as a weakness. This belief, ingrained from childhood, hinders his ability to have fulfilling relationships. Despite wanting to change, his subconscious belief that a "good man" does not show sensitivity prevents him from doing so.

The Challenge of Change

As people work on transforming their thoughts and lives, they often face resistance. This resistance usually stems from limiting beliefs. Most individuals are unaware of these beliefs; they only realize that making changes is difficult. Limiting beliefs reside in the subconscious mind and act as roadblocks to positive change. They are frequently formed from traumatic events in childhood and reinforced by negative experiences in adulthood.

Practical Exercises

1. **Emotional Reaction Journaling**: Keep a journal to record events that trigger strong emotional reactions. Reflect on these events to uncover possible limiting beliefs.
2. **Behavior Patterns Log**: Document your daily behaviors and look for patterns that might be self-defeating. Ask a trusted friend or family member to help you identify these patterns.
3. **Reflective Writing**: Write about significant events from your childhood that may have contributed to your current beliefs. This can help you understand the origin of your limiting beliefs.
4. **Affirmation Practice**: Create positive affirmations to counteract your limiting beliefs. Repeat them daily to help reprogram your subconscious mind.

By actively engaging in these exercises, you can begin to recognize and transform your limiting beliefs, paving the way for personal growth and a more fulfilling life.

Overcoming Negative Thought Patterns

Identifying Negative Thought Patterns

Negative thought patterns can be triggered by clear, identifiable events. However, more often than not, they are a buildup of various experiences, making it challenging to pinpoint their origins. This is why it is crucial to observe our automatic thoughts and identify the harmful ones. By writing them down as we notice them, we can often see how unfounded or irrational these thoughts are.

The Power of Negative Thoughts

Negative thoughts are powerful because they signify a divided mind—where the thinking self and the feeling self are not in agreement. Many people can relate to the sentiment of "a part of me believes this and a part of me doesn't." For instance, John may rationally conclude that he is intelligent, but he doesn't feel intelligent. This discrepancy exists because his negative thought pattern has been deeply ingrained and reinforced over time.

The Origin of Negative Thought Patterns

Negative thought patterns are self-critical beliefs that negatively impact our self-perception. These patterns often develop due to:

- **Negative Experiences in Childhood**: Traumatic or harmful experiences that shape our early beliefs about ourselves.
- **Detrimental Experiences in Adulthood**: Events or interactions that reinforce these early negative beliefs.
- **Inherited Messages**: Negative messages or beliefs passed down from parents or authority figures, often unintentionally.

Understanding that negative thinking was not deliberately taught but has nonetheless become deeply embedded is essential in addressing and overcoming these patterns.

Practical Exercises for Overcoming Negative Thoughts

1. **Automatic Thought Recording**: Keep a notebook handy and jot down any negative thoughts as they arise. Review these notes regularly to identify patterns and irrational beliefs.
2. **Rational Analysis**: Once you have identified a negative thought, challenge it by asking yourself:
     - Is this thought based on facts or feelings?
     - What evidence supports or contradicts this thought?
     - Is there an alternative, more balanced way of thinking about this situation?
3. **Mindfulness Practice**: Engage in mindfulness or meditation to become more aware of your thoughts and emotions without judgment. This can help you recognize negative patterns and respond more consciously.
4. **Positive Reframing**: Replace negative thoughts with positive or neutral alternatives. For example, instead of thinking "I always fail," reframe it to "I have had setbacks, but I am capable of learning and improving."

5. **Gratitude Journaling**: Each day, write down three things you are grateful for. This practice can shift your focus from negative to positive aspects of your life.

Understanding Negative Thought Patterns

Recognizing the presence and impact of negative thought patterns is the first step toward overcoming them. By consistently applying these exercises, you can begin to shift your thought processes and cultivate a more positive and empowering mindset.

CHAPTER 6

Cultivating Positive Thinking

The Power of Mental Imagery

With continued practice of mental imagery and focusing on positive outcomes, there is a significant shift in how one develops their skills. This practice enhances functional abilities, boosts self-motivation, and increases confidence in one's capabilities. By visualizing success, you set the stage for achieving it.

Transforming Thought Patterns

Changing your mindset from negative to positive has far-reaching effects. Enhanced performance, higher self-satisfaction, and the fulfillment of experiencing positive outcomes are some of the benefits. A positive mindset encourages:

- **Task Persistence**: The determination to keep going despite challenges.
- **Flexibility**: The ability to adapt to new situations and changes.
- **Recovery from Failure**: Bouncing back from setbacks with resilience.

- **Increased Creativity**: Opening the mind to innovative solutions and ideas.
- **Enhanced Problem-Solving**: Preparing the mind to tackle problems effectively, thereby influencing others' perceptions positively.

Practical Steps for Positive Thinking

1. **Draft a Realistic Statement**: Clearly define the situation, distinguishing between what is and what you wish it could be.
2. **Visualize Success**: Imagine a scenario where success is achieved. This visualization sets a strategic plan in motion to achieve your goals.
3. **Conscious Intention**: Evoke a conscious intention that a positive outcome will be realized. The more you practice this, the easier it becomes to produce enhanced performance and greater satisfaction.

The Mindset Shift

A positive mind anticipates happiness, joy, health, and success in every situation. Conversely, a negative mind expects failure and struggles to accept success, perpetuating a cycle of negativity.

Training the Mind

Positive thinking is achievable through mental training. Here are some exercises to cultivate a positive mindset:

1. **Surround Yourself with Positivity**: Eliminate negative influences from your environment. This creates space for constructive thoughts to flourish.

2. **Practice Gratitude**: Regularly note things you are grateful for. This shifts focus from what is lacking to what is abundant.
3. **Positive Affirmations**: Repeat affirmations that reinforce a positive self-image and outlook.
4. **Mindfulness and Meditation**: Engage in mindfulness or meditation to develop awareness and control over your thoughts.
5. **Positive Visualization**: Spend time each day visualizing positive outcomes in various areas of your life.

By consistently applying these practices, you can foster a positive mindset, making it easier to achieve your goals and experience greater satisfaction.

CHAPTER 7

Harnessing the Power of Affirmations

The Basics of Affirmations

Affirmations are powerful tools for manifesting your desires and achieving your goals. At its core, an affirmation is a declaration that something is true. When done correctly, affirmations can be a strong force in transforming your life. Think of an affirmation as planting a seed in your conscious or unconscious mind. With attention and nourishment, this thought-seed will grow and flourish.

The Alpha Mind State

To maximize the effectiveness of affirmations, it's beneficial to enter a receptive, alpha mind state. Alpha is a brainwave frequency between 7 and 14 cycles per second, a state of relaxed alertness often experienced during daydreaming, meditation, or when letting your mind wander.

Steps to Effective Affirmations

1. **Relaxation Technique**: Find a comfortable place to sit or lie down. Close your eyes and take several deep breaths to relax your body. Once relaxed, take three to five minutes to visualize your desired outcome. Use all your senses to make the vi-

sualization as real as possible. For example, if you desire a new romantic relationship, visualize receiving affection, spending quality time with a loving partner, and feeling happiness with another person. The more vivid the visualization, the faster it will manifest with the use of affirmation.

2. **State Your Affirmation**: After visualizing your desired manifestation, clearly state your affirmation. For instance, "I am attracting a loving and fulfilling relationship." Then, let go of it with the confidence that it is on the way.

3. **Planting the Seed**: The best way to plant the affirmation seed is to be in a relaxed, receptive state of mind. This can be achieved through meditation or any activity that helps you reach the alpha state. In this state, your mind is more open and receptive to positive suggestions.

Practical Exercises

1. **Daily Affirmation Practice**: Set aside time each day to practice your affirmations. Ensure you are in a relaxed state and fully immerse yourself in the visualization process.

2. **Affirmation Journal**: Keep a journal where you write down your affirmations and the feelings associated with them. Review and reflect on your progress regularly.

3. **Visualization Board**: Create a vision board with images and words that represent your affirmations. Place it somewhere you will see it daily to reinforce your positive thoughts.

4. **Affirmation Reminder**: Set reminders on your phone or place notes around your environment to prompt you to repeat your affirmations throughout the day.

The Impact of Positive Thinking

A positive mind anticipates happiness, joy, health, and successful outcomes in every situation. Conversely, a negative mind expects failure and often struggles to accept success, perpetuating a cycle of negativity. Positive thinking, fostered through affirmations, can translate thoughts and hopes into reality.

By consistently practicing these exercises, you will cultivate a positive mindset, making it easier to achieve your goals and experience greater satisfaction.

CHAPTER 8

Visualizing Your Desired Future

The Power of Visualization

Visualization is a powerful method for shaping your desired future. By consciously creating a mental image of a desired outcome, you can change habits, thought, and behavior patterns, even transforming aspects of who you are. Visualization helps your subconscious mind accept these new outcomes as reality, making it easier to achieve your goals.

Rewriting Past Experiences

Consider a time when you felt defeated, perhaps after not being selected for a job or sports team. Picture that moment and remember how it felt. Now, shake that image out of your mind and reimagine the same event, but this time visualize yourself achieving your goal. Imagine the smiles and congratulations from others, and feel the positive emotions associated with this success.

This process, known as "rewriting the past," doesn't change the actual event but alters how you feel about it. With practice, you can use this method to let go of past negative experiences and change your emotional response to them.

How the Brain Works

The brain is made up of nerve cells connected by pathways. The more you think a thought, the more it becomes a deep-set pattern as the connecting cells and pathways become thicker. Negative thought patterns or memories of past events are just deep-set pathways. When you use visualization to picture a new outcome, you are firing new impulses that create new connections and pathways. Repeating this new thought pattern reinforces it, eventually creating a new habit or permanent change.

Practical Steps for Effective Visualization

1. **Relaxation Technique**: Find a comfortable place to sit or lie down. Close your eyes and take several deep breaths to relax your body. Once relaxed, spend three to five minutes visualizing your desired outcome. Use all your senses to make the visualization as vivid as possible. For example, if you desire a new romantic relationship, visualize receiving affection, spending quality time with a loving partner, and experiencing happiness. The more real you make it, the faster it will manifest with the use of affirmation.

2. **State Your Affirmation**: After visualizing your desired manifestation, clearly state your affirmation. For instance, "I am attracting a loving and fulfilling relationship." Then, let go of it, knowing that it is on the way.

3. **Emotional Involvement**: The more emotion you put into the visualization, the more impact it will have. Your subconscious mind doesn't know the difference between a vividly imagined thought and reality. If you have a fear or phobia, it's because you've visualized the feared thing so many times that it has become very real in your mind. By visualizing positive outcomes with strong emotions, you can reverse this process and use it to achieve what you desire.

Practical Exercises

1. **Daily Visualization Practice**: Set aside time each day for visualization. Ensure you are in a relaxed state and fully immerse yourself in the visualization process.
2. **Visualization Journal**: Keep a journal where you write down your visualizations and the emotions associated with them. Review and reflect on your progress regularly.
3. **Vision Board**: Create a vision board with images and words that represent your visualizations. Place it somewhere you will see it daily to reinforce your positive thoughts.
4. **Visualization Reminder**: Set reminders on your phone or place notes around your environment to prompt you to practice visualization throughout the day.

By consistently practicing these exercises, you can harness the power of visualization to create a positive and fulfilling future.

CHAPTER 9

The Role of Mindfulness in Transforming Thoughts

The Basics of Mindfulness

Mindfulness meditation is a powerful tool for managing our thoughts and emotions. By practicing mindfulness, we become more skilled at observing our thoughts and deciding how to respond to them. Sometimes, a specific thought will pop into our mind unwanted, and we might try to actively get rid of it. With practice, it becomes easier to direct our attention away from unhelpful thoughts. Other times, simply watching the thought and seeing it for what it is can be more effective.

Mindfulness and the Present Moment

Mindfulness also brings a relaxed, full attention to the present moment. This increases the likelihood that our thinking will be based on an accurate assessment of reality. When we recognize that a particular thought pattern has led to unwanted actions or emotional states, we can practice mindfulness during the post-mortem—paying close attention to what triggered the thought and what we can do differently next time. With continued practice, these strategies become habitual, and the mind becomes a much easier place to reside.

Mindfulness as a Metacognitive Skill

In cognitive therapy, mindfulness is considered a metacognitive skill—a way of "thinking about thinking" that promotes cognitive and emotional well-being. By paying attention to our thought processes and cultivating an open and nonjudgmental perspective, we create the possibility of changing our thinking.

Deepening Awareness

Mindfulness helps us recognize the repetitive and self-judging nature of our thoughts. The more we practice, the more we can observe our thoughts without identifying with them or believing they tell the literal truth. Over time, this de-automatization of the thinking process allows us to see our thoughts with greater clarity and manage them more effectively.

Practical Exercises for Mindfulness

1. **Mindfulness Meditation**: Set aside time each day to practice mindfulness meditation. Sit comfortably, close your eyes, and focus on your breath. When thoughts arise, observe them without judgment and gently bring your attention back to your breath.

2. **Body Scan**: Lie down or sit comfortably and focus on each part of your body, from your toes to your head. Notice any sensations or tensions and observe them without trying to change anything. This practice helps increase body awareness and promote relaxation.

3. **Mindful Observation**: Spend a few minutes each day observing your surroundings with full attention. Notice the colors, shapes, sounds, and textures around you. This practice helps ground you in the present moment.

4. **Thought Watching**: When a negative or unhelpful thought arises, observe it without judgment. Acknowledge the thought, but do not engage with it or try to push it away. Simply watch it pass by like a cloud in the sky.

5. **Mindfulness Journal**: Keep a journal where you record your mindfulness experiences and reflections. Note any patterns or insights that emerge from your practice.

By incorporating these exercises into your daily routine, you can cultivate mindfulness and transform your thought patterns, leading to greater emotional well-being and cognitive clarity.

CHAPTER 10

Practicing Gratitude for a Positive Mindset

The Power of Gratitude

Gratitude has a profound influence on your mindset. It's challenging to feel sorry for yourself when you focus on the aspects of life for which you are grateful. Practicing gratitude regularly can lead to increased happiness, improved relationships, and a more positive outlook on life.

How to Practice Gratitude

1. **Gratitude List**: Make a list of all the things in your life that you are grateful for—people, possessions, opportunities, achievements. Regularly updating and reviewing this list can help maintain a positive mindset.
2. **Gratitude Journal**: Record your gratitude list in a journal. Spend a few minutes each day writing down what you are grateful for and reflect on how this changes your mood.
3. **Gratitude Triggers**: Set up 'gratitude triggers'—recurring events or times that remind you to consider what you are grateful for. For instance, think about a particular issue every

time you receive a gift, at meal times, or each morning after waking up.

4. **Gratitude Letters**: Write letters of thanks and appreciation to those who have helped you in life. Deliver these letters in person and read them aloud to the recipients. This practice strengthens relationships, boosts your happiness, and significantly enhances someone else's day.

Increasing Awareness

Make a conscious effort to avoid taking your current circumstances for granted. Imagine how your life would be if those things were taken away from you. This practice can make you more likely to appreciate what you have while you still have it.

Practical Exercises for Gratitude

1. **Five-Minute Gratitude Reflection**: Spend five minutes each day reflecting on the things you are grateful for. Notice how your mood lightens during this time.
2. **Gratitude Rituals**: Establish daily rituals to express gratitude. For example, during meals, share something you are grateful for with family or friends.
3. **Thank You Notes**: Write thank you notes for small acts of kindness you receive. This small gesture can have a big impact on your relationships and your mindset.
4. **Visual Reminders**: Place visual reminders around your home or workspace that prompt you to think about what you are grateful for.

By consistently practicing these exercises, you can cultivate a mindset of gratitude, leading to a more positive and fulfilling life.

CHAPTER 11

Embracing Self-Compassion and Self-Love

Understanding Self-Compassion

Self-compassion involves being kind to ourselves when life doesn't go as planned. Instead of mercilessly judging and criticizing ourselves for various inadequacies or shortcomings, self-compassion means being kind and understanding when confronted with personal failings. Recognizing that life is a long journey with many hardships, it is crucial to allow ourselves kindness and patience.

The Practice of Self-Compassion

To cultivate self-compassion, we must learn to treat ourselves as we would treat a good friend. This means providing our hearts with the sympathy and care needed when in pain. Being mindful of our emotions and understanding that it is okay to feel upset and angry about unwanted situations is essential. Then, we can be kind to ourselves in the midst of our sorrow.

Benefits of Self-Compassion

High levels of self-compassion have been directly linked to greater emotional well-being, less anxiety and depression, maintenance of healthy habits such as diet and exercise, and more satisfying personal relationships.

Practical Exercises for Self-Compassion

1. **Self-Compassionate Letter**: Write a letter to yourself from the perspective of a compassionate friend. Address your struggles and offer kind words and support.
2. **Mindful Self-Reflection**: Set aside time each day for mindful self-reflection. Acknowledge your emotions without judgment and offer yourself kindness and understanding.
3. **Positive Self-Talk**: Replace self-critical thoughts with positive self-talk. Practice phrases like "I am doing my best," "I deserve kindness," and "I am worthy of love."
4. **Self-Care Routine**: Develop a self-care routine that includes activities that bring you joy and relaxation. This could be anything from taking a bath, reading a book, or going for a walk.
5. **Gratitude Practice**: Incorporate gratitude into your daily routine by acknowledging the positive aspects of yourself and your life.

Cultivating Self-Love

Embracing self-compassion leads to a deeper sense of self-love. By consistently practicing self-compassion, we create a foundation for a positive and nurturing relationship with ourselves. This, in turn, enhances our emotional well-being and helps us develop healthier and more fulfilling relationships with others.

CHAPTER 12

Building Resilience in the Face of Challenges

Understanding Resilience

Fear of failure is one of the most common sources of anxiety. When your well-being is tied to the positive outcome of every endeavor, you might avoid taking on tasks where success is not guaranteed. This cautious approach can lead to an unsatisfying life. Developing realistic expectations for yourself and recognizing your capabilities are key steps in building resilience.

Embracing Human Fallibility

Remember, you are only human, and humans are fallible. Everyone makes mistakes and has shortcomings—this is what unites us. The goal is to do your best because that is all you can realistically ask of yourself. Your best is not a constant level; it fluctuates based on various factors such as how much sleep you got and what else is going on in your life.

Keeping Things in Perspective

It's perfectly okay to lower the bar for minor tasks. Keeping things in perspective helps prevent the escalation of failures and challenges. Though a setback may seem catastrophic at the moment, ask yourself how important it will be in the long run. Consider the advice you would offer a friend in a similar situation. Resilience involves managing distress healthily, not avoiding it.

Maintaining Healthy Routines

In times of high stress, it is crucial to pay extra attention to your well-being. This is when healthy routines are most important but often the first to go. Ensure you are eating right, exercising, and getting enough sleep. Many people mistakenly turn to alcohol, food, and other substances to cope with stress, which often backfires and exacerbates the problem.

Seeking Social Support

Instead of withdrawing from social supports, talk with friends and family about what you are going through. Sharing your experiences can provide relief and perspective. Sometimes, finding humor in the situation can help you view it as a learning experience. Learn how others with similar challenges have coped.

Cognitive Distortions and Therapy

The way we interpret events in our lives greatly impacts our resilience. Cognitive distortions can impair our ability to cope with difficult situations. Cognitive behavioral therapy (CBT) is an effective method for changing maladaptive ways of thinking. Many resilient people naturally use effective strategies without realizing it. Observe these individuals and try to incorporate their successful strategies into your own life.

Practical Exercises for Building Resilience

1. **Self-Compassion Exercise**: Practice self-compassion by treating yourself with the same kindness and understanding you would offer a friend.
2. **Mindfulness Meditation**: Engage in mindfulness meditation to develop awareness and acceptance of your thoughts and emotions.

3. **Gratitude Journal**: Keep a gratitude journal to remind your-self of the positive aspects of your life.
4. **Healthy Routine Checklist**: Create a checklist to ensure you are maintaining healthy routines, especially during stress-ful times.
5. **Social Support Network**: Identify and reach out to your support network when you need help. Don't be afraid to ask for assistance or share your struggles.

By consistently practicing these exercises, you can build resilience and navigate life's challenges with greater ease and confidence.

CHAPTER 13

Nurturing Healthy Relationships

Identifying Key Relationships

Identifying the key relationships in your life is essential for knowing where to focus your effort. Look for relationships that are important, supportive, and encourage personal growth. Importantly, identify those relationships that are not draining. Once identified, focus on maintaining and nurturing these connections. This may involve scheduling weekly dinners with friends or making regular phone calls to parents or siblings who live far away. The form of contact matters little; it's the effort and consistent attention to these relationships that makes a difference.

Communication

Effective communication is crucial in nurturing healthy relationships. Express your thoughts and feelings openly and honestly, and encourage others to do the same. Active listening, empathy, and understanding play significant roles in building trust and deepening connections.

Maintaining Balance

Maintaining the right balance in your life is key to healthy relationships. Ensure that you are giving enough time and energy to your important relationships without neglecting your own needs. Setting aside time for self-care enhances your relationship with yourself and allows you to be more present and supportive in your relationships with others.

Practical Steps for Nurturing Relationships

1. **Scheduled Quality Time**: Make a deal with a friend to schedule weekly dinners or regular phone calls with family members. Consistent contact helps strengthen bonds.

2. **Express Appreciation**: Regularly express gratitude and appreciation for the people in your life. Simple acts of kindness and acknowledgment can significantly enhance relationships.

3. **Active Listening**: Practice active listening by fully engaging in conversations, showing empathy, and responding thoughtfully. This fosters a deeper understanding and connection.

4. **Conflict Resolution**: Address conflicts and misunderstandings promptly and constructively. Focus on finding solutions rather than assigning blame.

5. **Support Personal Growth**: Encourage and support the personal and professional growth of those you care about. Celebrate their achievements and offer assistance when needed.

Self-Care and Independence

To nurture healthy relationships, it is vital to take care of yourself. Set aside time for activities that bring you joy and relaxation. Recognize that humans are interdependent, and a healthy relationship with yourself contributes to the quality of your relationships with others.

Building and Maintaining Quality Relationships

Building and maintaining quality relationships requires time, effort, and dedication. Recognize and believe that humans are naturally interdependent creatures. This interconnectedness helps us understand the significance of relationships in our lives.

By consistently practicing these steps and focusing on key areas, you can nurture healthy relationships that provide both personal and professional growth.

CHAPTER 14

Creating a Supportive Environment

Aligning Your Environment with Your Growth
When making changes to environments outside the home, it's essential to ensure that the new setting better aligns with who you are becoming and resonates with your new thoughts and ways of being. For instance, if certain environments were connected with the person you used to be or are tied to negative past experiences, it can be liberating to disassociate from those places and create new connections that reflect your internal changes.

Changing Social and Vocational Environments

This may involve changing social environments or even vocations. It's not about running away from anything but rather about letting go in a spacious manner to allow new experiences to come in. Be conscious not to leave gaps with the intention of avoiding anything; it's healthier to fill those gaps and create new experiences. The emphasis is on leading life forward, not backward. Letting go and embracing change can sometimes seem daunting, but it's important to focus on what is to be gained from these changes, putting the emphasis on potential and possibility.

Enhancing Physical Environments

Transformation can occur effortlessly and elegantly when we manage our thoughts wisely. To further support embracing new thoughts and ways of being, it can be extremely helpful to create a supportive physical environment. Here are some practical steps to enhance your environment:

1. **Decluttering**: Clear out items that no longer serve you or are tied to negative memories. This creates space for new, positive energy.

2. **Personalizing Spaces**: Decorate your living and working spaces with items that inspire you and reflect your new mindset. Use colors, artwork, and objects that promote positivity and growth.

3. **Creating Calm Areas**: Designate areas in your home or workspace for relaxation and mindfulness practices. Having a calm space can help you manage stress and stay centered.

4. **Incorporating Nature**: Bring elements of nature into your environment, such as plants or natural light. Nature has a calming effect and can boost your mood and creativity.

5. **Supportive Social Circles**: Surround yourself with people who support and encourage your growth. Build a social circle that aligns with your values and aspirations.

Practical Exercises for Creating a Supportive Environment

1. **Environment Audit**: Take a thorough audit of your current environments (home, work, social) and identify areas that no longer serve your growth. Make a plan to modify or move away from these areas.

2. **Vision Board**: Create a vision board that represents the new environments you want to create. Include images, words, and symbols that inspire you and align with your goals.
3. **Routine Changes**: Implement small changes in your daily routines to reinforce the new environments. This could include new habits like morning walks, meditation, or creative activities.
4. **Support Networks**: Actively seek out and engage with support networks, such as groups or communities that share your interests and goals.

Embracing Change

Change can be scary, but focusing on the potential and possibilities it brings can make the process more manageable. By consciously creating and maintaining supportive environments, you enhance your journey of transformation and ensure that your surroundings reflect and support your new ways of being.

CHAPTER 15

Maintaining Consistency in Thought Transformation

The Importance of Consistency

All the work done to shape and reshape your thoughts can be undone if you revert to old patterns. Maintaining consistency in supporting the mental changes you have diligently worked on is crucial. Once you have successfully adopted a new line of thinking, it is essential to stay consistent in your efforts to progress in this new direction.

Momentum in Thought Patterns

Thoughts are closely linked, and one thought often leads to another. Spending time on a particular plane of thinking creates momentum, which must be maintained to continue progressing in the same direction. For example, shifting from a sedentary lifestyle to a more active one involves a change in thought patterns. The decision to adopt healthier habits likely involved envisioning a healthier state and considering how to make the transition. Lasting changes in behavior are driven by a vivid comparison of present and envisioned future states. Reverting to old thought patterns can halt this progression.

Balancing Consistency and Flexibility

While consistency is crucial, attempting to forcefully hold thoughts can be counterproductive. Thought is a continuous process, and even a seemingly passive state involves some movement. Trying to maintain a given thought forcefully can create resistance and tension, hindering change. It is important to differentiate between the necessity of consistency and the need for constant conscious effort to maintain a thought. The latter often dissipates crucial changes.

Practical Steps for Maintaining Consistency

1. **Regular Reflection**: Set aside time each day to reflect on your new thought patterns and how they align with your goals. This practice helps reinforce the changes you have made.

2. **Mindfulness Practices**: Engage in mindfulness or meditation to stay aware of your thoughts and prevent slipping back into old patterns. This helps maintain a balanced and flexible mindset.

3. **Positive Reinforcement**: Celebrate your progress and reward yourself for maintaining consistency. Positive reinforcement can motivate you to keep going.

4. **Supportive Environment**: Surround yourself with people and environments that support your new way of thinking. This external support can help you stay consistent.

5. **Visual Reminders**: Use visual cues like sticky notes, vision boards, or digital reminders to keep your goals and new thought patterns in focus.

Embracing Change

Change can be intimidating, but focusing on the potential and possibilities it brings can make the process more manageable. By consciously creating and maintaining supportive environments, you enhance your journey of transformation and ensure that your surroundings reflect and support your new ways of being.

Taking Action: Applying Mind Transformation Techni

The Importance of Consistent Practice

Understanding how mind transformation techniques work is just the beginning. The key to their effectiveness lies in consistent practice and application. Many people tend to use these exercises only during times of stress, pain, or negative emotions. This is similar to half-heartedly learning a musical instrument and expecting to perform well at a recital. It's absolutely essential to practice these techniques regularly from the start, making moments of clarity and peace more accessible when needed.

Daily Practices for Mind Transformation

1. **Reflective Journal Writing**: Commit to writing about positive aspects of your life 3 to 5 times per week. This practice helps reinforce positive thinking and allows you to track your progress.

2. **Mind Visualization Exercise**: Perform daily visualization exercises focusing on desired outcomes for various events, is-

sues, or problems. Visualizing success and positive outcomes can help rewire your thought patterns.

3. **Mind Substitution Exercise**: Daily practice of substituting negative thoughts with positive ones. Identify a positive aspect and focus on it to gradually replace old thought patterns.

Measuring Progress

Gauge the efficacy and rate of improvement by noting how long positive feelings are sustained during and after the exercises. The mind tends to revert to ingrained patterns formed by lifelong experiences. Therefore, repetition is crucial for creating lasting change.

Building New Thought Pathways

Creating new thought patterns is akin to deviating the course of a mighty river. Just as it would take 60-90 days of consistent effort to carve a new route for the Mississippi River, it takes persistent practice to establish new mental pathways. Recognize that it took years of experiences to form your current thought patterns, and be patient with the process.

Practical Exercises for Consistency

1. **Daily Practice Schedule**: Create a daily schedule for your mind transformation exercises. Consistency is key to making these practices a habit.

2. **Progress Tracker**: Use a progress tracker to monitor your daily practice and note any changes in your thought patterns and emotional state.

3. **Mindfulness Reminders**: Set reminders to engage in mindfulness practices throughout the day. This helps maintain awareness and prevents slipping back into old patterns.

4. **Support System**: Share your goals with a friend or family member who can provide support and accountability. Having someone to encourage you can make a significant difference.

5. **Regular Reviews**: Schedule regular reviews of your progress and adjust your practices as needed. Celebrate your successes and learn from any setbacks.

Embracing Change

Embracing mind transformation requires dedication and patience. By maintaining consistency and practicing regularly, you can create lasting positive changes in your thought patterns and overall well-being.